# E. B. White

## My Favorite Writer

**Rennay Craats**

WEIGL PUBLISHERS INC.

Published by Weigl Publishers Inc.
123 South Broad Street, Box 227
Mankato, MN 56002
USA
Web site: www.weigl.com

Library of Congress Cataloging-in-Publication Data

Craats, Rennay.
  E.B. White / Rennay Craats.
      p. cm. -- (My favorite writer)
Summary: A biography of American author E.B. White, who is best known for writing "Charlotte's Web," plus a chapter of creative writing tips.
  ISBN 1-59036-026-5 (lib. bdg. : alk. paper)
 1. White, E. B. (Elwyn Brooks), 1899---Juvenile literature.
2.Authors, American--20th century--Biography--Juvenile literature.
3.Children's stories--Authorship--Juvenile literature. [1. White, E. B. (Elwyn Brooks), 1899- 2. Authors, American. 3. Authorship.] I. Title. II. Series.
  PS3545.H5187 Z616 2002
  818'.5209--dc21

                                                    2002005585

**Editor**
Jennifer Nault

**Copy Editor**
Heather Kissock

**Design and Layout**
Terry Paulhus

**Photo Researcher**
Tina Schwartzenberger

Printed in Canada
1 2 3 4 5 6 7 8 9 10  06 05 04 03 02

# Contents

# E. B. White

# MILESTONES

**1899** Born on July 11, in Mount Vernon, New York

**1911** Wins writing contest for his story "A Winter Walk," which is published in a children's journal

**1921** Graduates from Cornell University

**1926** Joins the staff of *The New Yorker* magazine

**1929** Marries *The New Yorker* fiction editor Katharine Angell and publishes his first collection of poetry

**1938** Moves to a farm in Maine

**1945** *Stuart Little* is published

**1952** *Charlotte's Web* is published

**1970** *The Trumpet of the Swan* is published

**1977** Katharine Angell White passes away

**1985** E. B. White dies after a lengthy battle with **Alzheimer's disease**

Growing up would not be the same without the wonderful tales by author Elwyn Brooks White, better known as E. B. White. Children love to read about Stuart Little's adventures, Charlotte's clever plans to save Wilbur the pig, and Louis the swan's trumpet playing. E. B. White's children's books are classics. They are read in schools and homes across the country.

At the beginning of his career, children were not E. B.'s main readers. He made a living writing essays for adults that were published in newspapers and magazines. He also wrote popular books of poetry. E. B. began writing children's stories to entertain his son, nieces, and nephews. His stories, which amused his family, also delighted millions of young readers around the world. E. B. White's stories are timeless.

Today, many of his early fans have grown up. Many are still reading E. B. White's books—to their own children. E. B. wrote only three children's novels during his writing career. Those three books have made him a legend in children's **literature**.

# Early Childhood

Of Samuel and Lillian White's six children, Elwyn Brooks White was the youngest. E. B. was born on July 11, 1899, in Mount Vernon, New York. His father was the owner of a piano manufacturing company. The White's large farmhouse was filled with love and happiness. However, this did not always keep young E. B. from worrying. From the darkness of the attic to his future, E. B. worried about everything.

One of E. B.'s greatest worries was of public speaking. When he was a young student, everyone who attended E. B.'s school had to present a poem or a speech in front of an audience. E. B. worried about reading his assignment aloud. He thought the other students would laugh at him. At times, E. B.'s fear of public speaking was so great that he would just run off the stage. E. B. would try to coax other students into reading his poems and speeches in his place. The fear of public speaking never left E. B. White.

E. B. White's birthplace, Mount Vernon, is located in the metropolitan area of New York City.

Growing up on a farm, E. B. was happiest when he was near animals. He took care of chicken's eggs and enjoyed watching baby chicks hatch. His dog, Mac, was never far from his side. E. B. often kept to himself. He liked to ride his bicycle, ice-skate, and canoe. He also liked to write. E. B. found it exciting to fill blank pages with his own words. It was then that E. B. overcame one of his biggest fears—what he would do for a living. He decided to become a writer.

E. B. was a good writer. When he was 11 years old, he wrote a poem about a mouse. The poem was published in a magazine. The following year, E. B.'s story "A Winter Walk" received top honors in a writing contest. It was published in the *St. Nicholas Magazine,* a children's journal. Whenever E. B. had spare time, he wrote poems and stories. They were about his life, his view of the world, and about animals. E. B. continued to be fascinated by these subjects for the rest of his life.

As a young child, E. B. White loved animals. It is not surprising that he wrote books about them.

# Growing Up

In high school, E. B. wrote essays about local and worldly issues for the school magazine.

Although E. B. White was a good student, he was motivated by more than just a love of learning. E. B. worked hard at school, partly out of fear. He was afraid of attracting the teachers' attention and of falling behind his classmates in his studies. In high school, E. B. wrote essays about local news and political issues for the school magazine. He also filled the role of assistant editor.

Meanwhile, Europe was on the brink of World War I. E. B. thought the United States should not go to war. Many of his essays expressed this opinion. In 1914, World War I began, and the United States supported the **Allies**. Although he was against his country's involvement, E. B. remained **patriotic**. He wanted to support his country. E. B. was too young to become a soldier, so he supported the war effort by working on farms belonging to farmers who were serving overseas. E. B. joined the army in 1918. He served as a private before returning to New York to attend Cornell University in Ithaca.

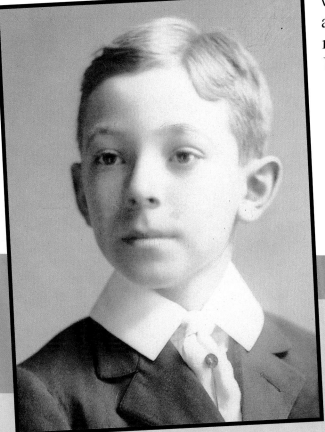

E. B. White attended public school in Mount Vernon.

8

In E. B. White's first year at Cornell University, he wrote for the university newspaper. Since he had not yet outgrown his shyness, E. B. thought that joining a **fraternity** might help him become bolder, and it did. His fraternity brothers called him Andy because he had the same last name as the school's president, Andrew White. The name stuck, and people called him Andy for the rest of his life. E. B. was elected president of his fraternity in his junior year at Cornell University. Despite his popularity, E. B. did not forget about his writing. He was named head editor of the university's daily newspaper.

William Strunk, Jr., an English professor at Cornell University, taught E. B. how to craft his writing. William Strunk, Jr. is best known for his writer's guidebook *The Elements of Style*. E. B. graduated from Cornell University in 1921. By that time, he had written more than 180 **editorials** for the university newspaper.

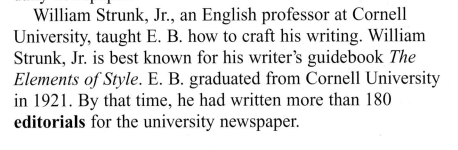

# Inspired to Write

E. B. White began writing as a young boy. Although he loved to write, he had to work very hard at it. An English professor gave E. B. advice that influenced his writing. He told E. B. that every sentence is like a boat. One ill-suited word can sink it. After receiving that advice, E. B. worked toward writing clearly and simply.

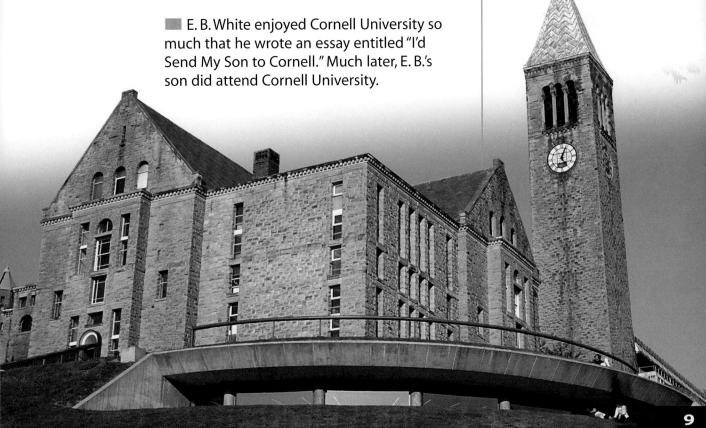

■ E. B. White enjoyed Cornell University so much that he wrote an essay entitled "I'd Send My Son to Cornell." Much later, E. B.'s son did attend Cornell University.

After he graduated, E. B. felt that he was ready to tackle the "real world," but settling down was not as easy as he thought. E. B. and a school friend, Howard Cushman, decided to travel for a while. E. B. gathered a few things and packed them into his automobile. Without a fixed destination or very much money, the two started driving across the United States. They wrote short articles for magazines along the way and found odd jobs to pay for gas and food. E. B. and Howard worked on farms, played piano, and washed dishes to fund their travels. They ended up in Seattle, Washington, and E. B. decided to stay there. He found a job reporting for the *Seattle Times*, where he worked for one year.

E. B.'s next adventure was a six-week cruise to Alaska. He could not afford the trip, so he found a job working in the ship's **mess hall**. When the trip was over, E. B. returned home to focus on his writing career.

E. B. White wrote articles for his university newspaper, the *Cornell Daily Sun*.

# Favorite Authors

E. B.'s favorite author was Henry David Thoreau. Thoreau was a well-known American writer and **philosopher**. In the mid-1800s, Thoreau lived in a small, remote hut on Walden Pond near Concord, Massachusetts. He moved there to study nature, read great works, and mingle with local residents. It was Thoreau's devotion to nature and the simple life that drew E. B. to his writing. E. B. once said that Thoreau's book *Walden* was the only book he owned.

At the age of 22, E. B. returned to the state of New York and moved in with his parents. He was not sure where to look for writing jobs. A **literary** magazine called *The New Yorker* caught E. B.'s eye when it first came to newsstands. He admired the quality of writing, so he began submitting articles. Within a few months, *The New Yorker* began publishing his articles. Before long, people all over the country were reading his words.

Over the next forty years, E. B. became an important part of *The New Yorker*. He wrote essays, poems, stories, and news pieces. While working for *The New Yorker*, E. B. met and fell in love with the magazine's editor, Katharine Angell. They were married in 1929. Two years later, they had a son, Joel. Seven years after that, the Whites moved to a farm in Maine. In Maine, E. B. continued to write for *The New Yorker* and other literary magazines.

Although E. B. and his wife, Katharine, worked together at *The New Yorker*, she never edited E. B. 's writing. He would not let her see his work until it was finished.

# Learning the Craft

E. B. White had never thought about writing children's literature. He did not consider himself to be a storyteller.

Although he was an **established** essay writer, E. B. had never thought about writing children's literature. He certainly did not consider himself to be a storyteller. However, his son Joel, and numerous nieces and nephews, began asking E. B. to tell them stories. He made up imaginative stories for them. The children would ask to hear their favorite stories again and again. Sometimes E. B. would forget some details of his stories. He starting writing them down to remember them.

One of the characters in E. B.'s stories was a little mouse named Stuart Little. The amusing story idea came to E. B. while he was sleeping on a train. He did not write the tale until ten years later. Writing the story was more difficult than he thought it would be. It was a challenge for him to sit and write for long periods of time. However, E. B. kept working at it and finished the book in 1945. *Stuart Little* was a great success, making E. B. White a famous children's author.

The 1999 movie *Stuart Little* is based on E. B. White's well-loved book.

Over the years, E. B. continued to write **inspirational** books for children. In 1952, *Charlotte's Web* was published. It was a story about the friendship between a pig and a spider. E. B. spent several months researching spiders and animal behavior. He wanted to make the story believable and to get his characters just right. He based the book partly on his own experiences growing up on a farm, surrounded by animals. Once again, E. B.'s book was a great success. It earned him many awards and was translated into twenty different languages.

It was many years before children could begin reading a new E. B. White book. In 1970, he published *The Trumpet of the Swan*. E. B., who was a **perfectionist**, was not completely happy with the book. However, children and **critics** loved it. *The Trumpet of the Swan* earned E. B. several awards. Although he continued to write, *The Trumpet of the Swan* was his last children's novel.

## Inspired to Write

The **dynamic** environment of New York City served as the subject for many of E. B.'s essays. His interest in society inspired him to write about city life. He wrote about the things he liked and disliked about the world, society, and human nature. E. B.'s writing was very personal, and he often expressed his views in a humorous manner.

New York City, where E. B. White lived as a young writer, continues to inspire writers and artists today.

# Getting Published

When he sat down to write his first children's book, E. B. was already a well-known author. He spent many years thinking about the character Stuart Little before writing about the mouse's adventures. Finally, E. B. sent the completed **manuscript** to Harper & Row Publishers. The children's book editor of the company, Ursula Nordstrom, loved the story. She accepted the manuscript for publication. E. B. worked with artist Garth Williams on the illustrations for the book.

Still, not everyone liked the book. The head of children's literature at the New York Public Library raised concerns about the book. She believed that *Stuart Little* was missing a tidy, happy ending. She felt children would be disappointed if the story was left **open-ended**. Some people also thought that the story was too unbelievable. Despite criticism, the book was published.

# The Publishing Process

Publishing companies receive hundreds of manuscripts from authors each year. Only a few manuscripts become books. Publishers must be sure that a manuscript will sell many copies. As a result, publishers reject most of the manuscripts they receive.

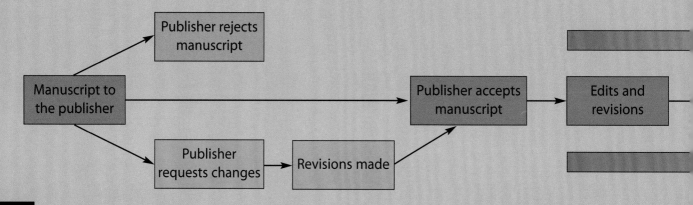

After the enormous success of *Stuart Little*, children and parents eagerly awaited E. B.'s next book. Even his publisher did not know that he was busy writing *Charlotte's Web*. E. B. had not discussed the book with anyone. One day, E. B. simply appeared at Harper & Row Publishers and handed Ursula an envelope. He left without saying a word. In the envelope was the manuscript for *Charlotte's Web*. Ursula could hardly believe how great the story was. After reading only a few chapters, she was convinced that E. B. had done it again.

*Charlotte's Web* was published in 1952. Today, it is known as one of the best children's books of all time. In 1970, *The Trumpet of the Swan* was published, much to the delight of E. B.'s loyal fans. Like his other two children's books, *The Trumpet of the Swan* quickly became a classic.

## Inspired to Write

E. B.'s love for animals and rural life inspired much of his writing. When E. B. was a child, Charlotte the spider from *Charlotte's Web* spun webs in the doorways of the family farmhouse. E. B. also fed a pig that was doomed to be slaughtered, just like Wilbur the pig. As an adult, the graceful swans at the Philadelphia Zoo inspired E. B. to write *The Trumpet of the Swan*.

Once a manuscript has been accepted, it goes through many stages before it is published. Often, authors change their work to follow an editor's suggestions. Once the book is published, some authors receive royalties. This is money based on book sales.

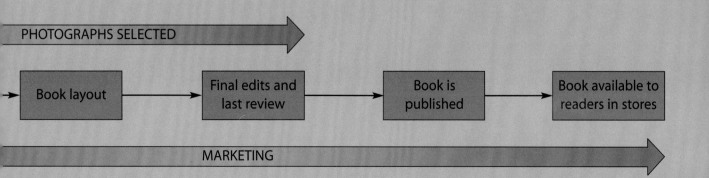

PHOTOGRAPHS SELECTED

Book layout → Final edits and last review → Book is published → Book available to readers in stores

MARKETING

# Writer Today

E. B. White rarely gave interviews and avoided award presentations.

Over the years, E. B. valued his privacy more and more. Sadly, Katharine Angell White died in 1977. After the loss of his wife, E. B. guarded his privacy. He rarely gave interviews and avoided award presentations. When he was given an award, he would send a written acceptance speech that the presenters could read to the crowd.

When E. B. retired, he lived permanently on his farm in Maine. There, he focused on what mattered most to him. He took care of his farm animals, canoed, and spent time with his family. E. B. lived a quiet and simple life during his retirement. The great writer passed away on October 1, 1985. E. B. died from an illness called Alzheimer's disease. He was 86 years old.

E. B. White loved the simple life that his farm in Maine offered. He spent his retirement days there, looking after his many farm animals.

The author's death saddened the entire nation. E. B.'s characters and stories touched adults and young people, not just in the United States, but around the globe. E. B.'s books have been an important part of growing up for many children. The author also inspired a great number of journalists and magazine writers, who remembered E. B. as the reason they started a writing career. E. B. White delighted and inspired people all over the world.

E. B.'s death did not affect readers' interest in his books. Long after the books were first published, children and adults continue to read these classic tales. In 1990, a nation-wide poll of the United States found that *Charlotte's Web* was still named the favorite book among children. Today, E. B. White is remembered as a wonderful essayist and a gifted storyteller.

■ *Charlotte's Web* was made into an animated movie in 1973.

# Popular Books

For years, E. B. White's wonderful stories have thrilled young readers. His books are entertaining and enjoyable. This section will provide you with brief introductions to some of E. B.'s most-loved books and the characters found within those books.

## AWARDS

**1963** Presidential Medal of Freedom

**1970** Laura Ingalls Wilder Award

**1971** National Medal for Literature

**1978** Pulitzer Prize special mention

## Charlotte's Web

In this story of friendship and hardship, E. B. White reminds readers that even simple things, such as a barnyard, can be filled with wonder. *Charlotte's Web* is set on a farm. When a litter of pigs is born, the farm owner decides to kill the **runt.** He thinks that it will likely die anyway. The farmer's daughter, Fern, begs him to let her raise the piglet.

Fern calls the little pig Wilbur and nurses him from a bottle until he grows strong. Before long, Wilbur the pig is too big for Fern to care for. She sells Wilbur to her uncle, Homer Zuckerman. His farm is just down the street, so Fern can still visit her friend. Wilbur misses Fern, but he is not lonely for long. A spider named Charlotte lives in the doorway of Wilbur's new pigpen. She becomes his best friend. Wilbur soon adds geese, sheep, and a rat named Templeton to his list of barnyard friends. When Fern comes by to visit, she sits on a stool and listens to the animals' conversations.

The barnyard fun is soon hampered by a terrible discovery: Wilbur's new owner, Homer, is planning to serve him for Christmas dinner. Poor Wilbur is very afraid. He does not want to die. Charlotte promises to save Wilbur from the Christmas feast. Charlotte's clever plan to save Wilbur and the adventures that follow will keep readers on the edge of their seats.

## AWARDS
### Charlotte's Web

**1953** Newbery Honor Book

**1958** Lewis Carroll Shelf Award

**1970** George C. Stone Center for Children's Books Recognition of Merit Award

**1973** New England Round Table of Children's Libraries Award

## Stuart Little

The Littles are a family with an extraordinary child. Their son, Stuart, is a mouse. Measuring only 2 inches tall, Stuart's small size leads him on many adventures. He is lowered into a bathtub drain to find a lost ring and chased by the family cat, Snowbell. Stuart even fixes the piano by squeezing himself between the key spaces. His size certainly does not stop him from having many great adventures. His greatest round of adventures begins when his best friend, a bird named Margalo, flies away from the Little's home. Margalo flies away because she is afraid that she will be eaten by Snowbell. Stuart leaves home in search of his friend. His transportation is a miniature car, which has a real gasoline-powered motor in it. Stuart Little meets interesting characters while on his quest. Some of the characters help Stuart out of sticky situations, while others get him into even bigger messes.

**AWARDS**
*Stuart Little*

**1970** Laura Ingalls Wilder Award

Actor Michael J. Fox was cast as the voice of Stuart in the motion picture *Stuart Little*.

## The Trumpet of the Swan

Louis is a trumpeter swan who cannot trumpet. One day, Louis meets Sam, a boy who tries to help him. Sam teaches Louis to communicate through reading and writing. Louis uses a chalkboard to write messages to those around him. Louis's father wants him to communicate with other swans as well. Although he knows his actions are wrong, Louis's father smashes the window of a music store and steals a trumpet. Louis learns to play the trumpet with great skill. Even though he is thankful for the trumpet, Louis feels guilty that his father stole it from the music store. He decides to find a job to pay back the owner of the music store. Louis has other plans, too. He wants to return home and win the heart of the beautiful female swan, Serena. This story is entertaining and fun, while teaching valuable life lessons.

**AWARDS**
*The Trumpet of the Swan*

**1972** International Board on Books for Young People Honor List
**1973** Children's Book Award
**1973** Sequoyah Children's Book Award
**1974** Sue Hefley Award from the Louisiana Association of School Librarians
**1975** Young Hoosier Award

# Creative Writing Tips

While writing is not always easy, the results are worth it. E. B. White followed certain rules when he wrote. These tips can help you improve your writing, too.

## Choice Words

As a young boy, E. B. spent a great deal of time flipping through the pages of his dictionary in search of great treasures—words. As an adult, he continued to improve his **vocabulary** by watching out for fascinating words. Words are the building blocks of any piece of writing. Having a good dictionary and using it is very important. Authors work hard to select the perfect word or to use an interesting word in place of a more common one.

## Write in a Journal

People keep a journal or diary for many reasons. Some people want to keep a record of everything that happens to them. For other people, having a journal allows them to keep track of their thoughts and feelings. E. B. started writing in a journal when he was 8 years old. He filled its pages with the day's events. He also overcame many of his fears by writing about them.

"I like animals, and my barn is a very pleasant place to be, at all hours!"
E. B. White

■ E. B. White wrote essays and poetry for *The New Yorker* for more than forty years.

## Over and Over Again

The key to good writing is rewriting. This step occurs after the completion of the first **draft** of a story. Many authors will revise their writing several times to make improvements. Even E. B. White, who started writing before he was a teenager, had to revise his writing. In fact, he rewrote the beginning of *Charlotte's Web* nine times before he was happy with it. That is why many writers publish only one book every few years. For many writers, it can take a long time to put the finishing touches on a story.

## Write What You Know

One way to come up with an idea for a story is to draw from real-life experiences. This does not mean that the story has to be completely true. For new writers, it is often easier to write about a familiar subject. E. B. White wrote about what he knew and loved best. If he did not know much about a subject, he would research it thoroughly.

## Comfort Level

Being comfortable can help one's ideas flow. Many writers follow a routine to ease themselves into their work. Some write at a certain time of day. Others require complete quiet or the sound of a radio playing softly in the background. Writers need to find out what routine works best for them. E. B. could write in the midst of noise and disruptions. Often, his children would run circles around his desk as he worked. However, E. B.'s work area was much like his writing style—clean and simple. E. B. kept his desk bare and set it near an open window. Keeping his desk clutter-free was important to him.

## Inspired to Write

E. B. White often wrote in an old boathouse, sitting on a wooden bench that was very uncomfortable. Spikes in the bench that poked into his back and swarms of insects kept distracting him. Eventually, E. B. built himself a better bench and put up a protective screen around the boathouse. These changes made work much easier.

# Writing a Biography Review

A biography is an account of an individual's life that is written by another person. Some people's lives are very interesting. In school, you may be asked to write a biography review. The first thing to do when writing a biography review is to decide whom you would like to learn about. Your school library or community library will have a large selection of biographies from which to choose.

Are you interested in an author, a sports figure, an inventor, a movie star, or a president? Finding the right book is your first task. Whether you choose to write your review on a biography of E. B. White or another person, the task will be similar.

Begin your review by writing the title of the book, the author, and the person featured in the book. Then, start writing about the main events in the person's life. Include such things as where the person grew up and what his or her childhood was like. You will want to add details about the person's adult life, such as whether he or she married or had children. Next, write about what you think makes this person special. What kinds of experiences influenced this individual? For instance, did he or she grow up in unusual circumstances? Was the person determined to accomplish a goal? Include any details that surprised you.

A concept web is a useful research tool. Use the concept web on the right to begin researching your biography review.

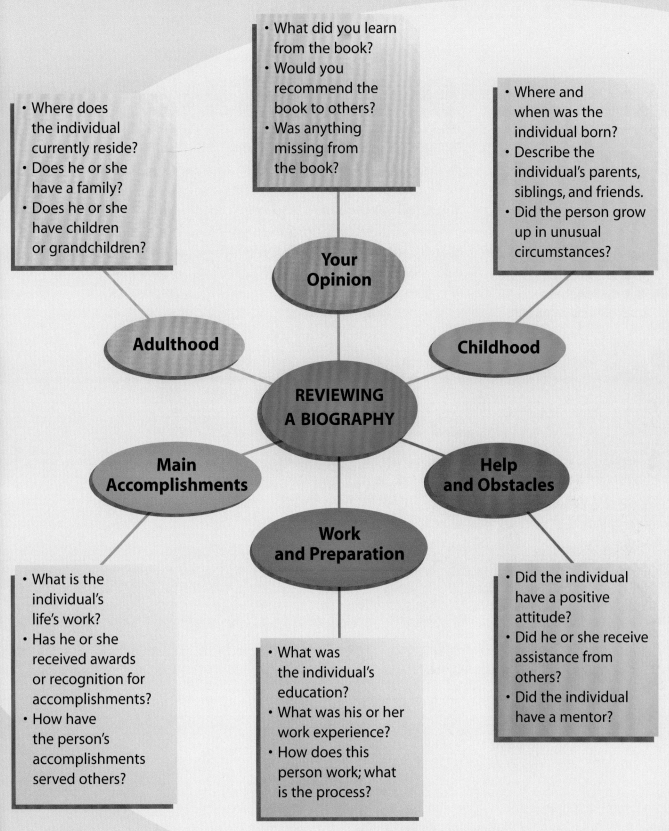

• Where does the individual currently reside?
• Does he or she have a family?
• Does he or she have children or grandchildren?

• What did you learn from the book?
• Would you recommend the book to others?
• Was anything missing from the book?

• Where and when was the individual born?
• Describe the individual's parents, siblings, and friends.
• Did the person grow up in unusual circumstances?

**Your Opinion**

**Adulthood**

**Childhood**

**REVIEWING A BIOGRAPHY**

**Main Accomplishments**

**Help and Obstacles**

**Work and Preparation**

• What is the individual's life's work?
• Has he or she received awards or recognition for accomplishments?
• How have the person's accomplishments served others?

• What was the individual's education?
• What was his or her work experience?
• How does this person work; what is the process?

• Did the individual have a positive attitude?
• Did he or she receive assistance from others?
• Did the individual have a mentor?

# Fan Information

People who want to experience E. B. White's stories have many ways to do so. After reading the books, fans can listen to voice recordings of the stories. There are even some recordings done by E. B. White himself. E. B. White made a tape recording of *Charlotte's Web* in 1973. The author's stories have also appeared on the small and big screens. *Stuart Little* was made into a television movie in 1966. It was then released as a full-length movie in 1999. *Charlotte's Web* was made into a cartoon movie in 1972 and a film in 1973.

E. B. White's farmhouse in North Brooklin, Maine was close to his family, including his grandchildren. This allowed them to spend time together.

Readers who enjoy E. B. White's books can find more information about him on the Internet. There are many Web sites that feature E. B.'s children's stories. Surfing the Internet is a great way to learn about this gifted author.

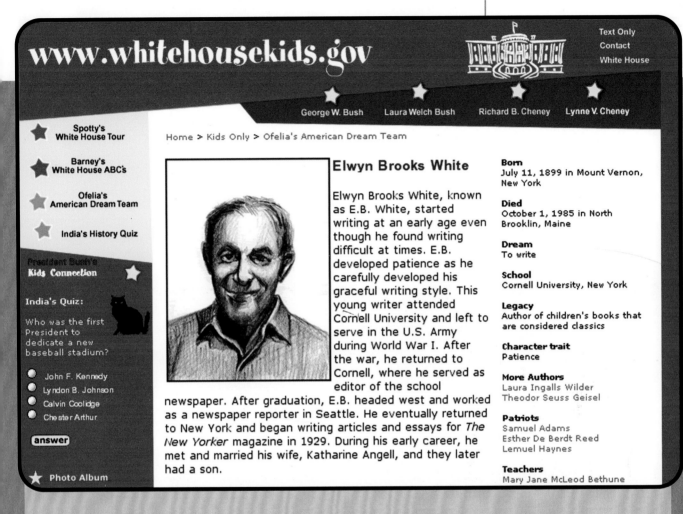

## www.whitehousekids.gov

Text Only
Contact
White House

George W. Bush    Laura Welch Bush    Richard B. Cheney    Lynne V. Cheney

Spotty's
White House Tour

Barney's
White House ABC's

Ofelia's
American Dream Team

India's History Quiz

President Bush's
Kids Connection

India's Quiz:

Who was the first President to dedicate a new baseball stadium?

○ John F. Kennedy
○ Lyndon B. Johnson
○ Calvin Coolidge
○ Chester Arthur

( answer )

★ Photo Album

Home > Kids Only > Ofelia's American Dream Team

### Elwyn Brooks White

Elwyn Brooks White, known as E.B. White, started writing at an early age even though he found writing difficult at times. E.B. developed patience as he carefully developed his graceful writing style. This young writer attended Cornell University and left to serve in the U.S. Army during World War I. After the war, he returned to Cornell, where he served as editor of the school newspaper. After graduation, E.B. headed west and worked as a newspaper reporter in Seattle. He eventually returned to New York and began writing articles and essays for *The New Yorker* magazine in 1929. During his early career, he met and married his wife, Katharine Angell, and they later had a son.

**Born**
July 11, 1899 in Mount Vernon, New York

**Died**
October 1, 1985 in North Brooklin, Maine

**Dream**
To write

**School**
Cornell University, New York

**Legacy**
Author of children's books that are considered classics

**Character trait**
Patience

**More Authors**
Laura Ingalls Wilder
Theodor Seuss Geisel

**Patriots**
Samuel Adams
Esther De Berdt Reed
Lemuel Haynes

**Teachers**
Mary Jane McLeod Bethune

## WEB LINKS

**Whitehousekids**

**www.whitehouse.gov/kids/dreamteam/elwynwhite.html**

Visitors to this Web site can read E. B. White's biography to learn more about the author.
Fans can also test their knowledge with a fun quiz.

**The Harper Childrens Web Site**

**www.harperchildrens.com/hch/author/author/white/**

Follow the links to find everything a fan of E. B. White could ask for, including puzzles and fascinating facts.

# Quiz

**Q:** Where was E. B. White born?

**1**

**A: E. B. White was born in Mount Vernon, New York.**

**2**

**Q:** How did E. B. White feel about speaking in public?

**A: E. B. had a great fear of public speaking.**

**3**

**Q:** After he finished high school, what university did E. B. attend?

**A: Cornell University in Ithaca, New York**

**Q:** Who was the Cornell University English professor that helped E. B. craft his writing?

**A: William Strunk, Jr.**

**Q:** What is the title of E. B.'s first children's book?

**A: Stuart Little**

**Q:** Where did E. B. White live during his retirement?

**A: E. B. stayed on his farm in Maine.**

**Q:** Who did E. B. White marry?

**A: Katharine Angell, editor of The New Yorker**

**Q:** Did noise bother E. B. White when he was writing?

**A: E. B. White had no problem working with noise in the background.**

**Q:** For what national literary magazine did E. B. work?

**A: The New Yorker**

**Q:** What is unique about the Little's son, Stuart?

**A: Stuart Little is a mouse.**

# Writing Terms

This glossary will introduce you to some of the main terms in the field of writing. Understanding these common writing terms will allow you to discuss your ideas about books and writing with others.

**action:** the moving events of a work of fiction

**antagonist:** the person in the story who opposes the main character

**autobiography:** a history of a person's life written by that person

**biography:** a written account of another person's life

**character:** a person in a story, poem, or play

**climax:** the most exciting moment or turning point in a story

**episode:** a short piece of action, or scene, in a story

**fiction:** stories about characters and events that are not real

**foreshadow:** hinting at something that is going to happen later in the book

**imagery:** a written description of a thing or idea that brings an image to mind

**narrator:** the speaker of the story who relates the events

**nonfiction:** writing that deals with real people and events

**novel:** published writing of considerable length that portrays characters within a story

**plot:** the order of events in a work of fiction

**protagonist:** the leading character of a story; often a likable character

**resolution:** the end of the story, when the conflict is settled

**scene:** a single episode in a story

**setting:** the place and time in which a work of fiction occurs

**theme:** an idea that runs throughout a work of fiction

# Glossary

**Allies:** the nations that fought against the Central Powers in World War I

**Alzheimer's disease:** a brain disorder that affects memory

**critics:** people whose job it is to say or write their opinions

**draft:** a first, rough version of a piece of writing

**dynamic:** having a great deal of energy and activity

**editorials:** articles in a newspaper, usually expressing the author's point of view

**established:** settled into a respectable position in one's business

**fraternity:** an organization made up of male university or college students

**inspirational:** something that serves to motivate

**literary:** relating to writing and books

**literature:** writing of lasting value, including plays, poems, and novels

**manuscript:** a draft of a story before it is published

**mess hall:** the place where the ship's crew eat in close quarters

**open-ended:** having no fixed answer or conclusion

**patriotic:** supporting and defending one's country and its interests

**perfectionist:** a person who demands a standard of excellence

**philosopher:** a deep thinker who studies the nature of life

**runt:** an undersized animal

**vocabulary:** all of the words used or understood by a person or group

# Index

# Photo Credits

Cover illustration by Terry Paulhus
Comstock, Inc.: page 13; Division of Rare & Manuscript Collections, Cornell University Library: pages 1, 4, 11, 22; Courtesy of HarperCollins Publishers: page 21; Map Resources: page 6; Manrico Mirabelli/MaXx Images: page 9; PhotoDisc, Inc.: page 28; Photofest: pages 3, 12, 17, 18, 20; Courtesy of Allene White: pages 7, 8, 10, 16, 26; www.whitehouse.gov/kids/dreamteam/elwynwhite.html: page 27.